St. Patrick's Day!

by Richard Sebra

LERNER PUBLICATIONS ◆ MINNEAPOLIS

Note to Educators:

Throughout this book, you'll find critical thinking questions. These can be used to engage young readers in thinking critically about the topic and in using the text and photos to do so.

Lerner Publications Company
A division of Lerner Publishing Group, Inc.
241 First Avenue North
Minneapolis, MN 55401 USA

For reading levels and more information, look up this title at www.lernerbooks.com.

Library of Congress Cataloging-in-Publication Data

Names: Sebra, Richard, 1984– author.
Title: It's St. Patrick's Day! / by Richard Sebra.
Other titles: It is Saint Patrick's Day!
Description: Minneapolis : Lerner Publications, [2016] | Series: Bumba Books — It's a Holiday! | Includes
    bibliographical references and index. | Audience: Ages: 4–8. | Audience: Grades: K to Grade 3.
Identifiers: LCCN 2016018670 (print) | LCCN 2016028640 (ebook) | ISBN 9781512425611 (lb : alk. paper) |
    ISBN 9781512429190 (pb : alk. paper) | ISBN 9781512427400 (eb pdf)
Subjects: LCSH: Saint Patrick's Day—Juvenile literature.
Classification: LCC GT4995.P3 S43 2016 (print) | LCC GT4995.P3 (ebook) | DDC 394.262—dc23

LC record available at https://lccn.loc.gov/2016018670

Manufactured in the United States of America
1 – VP – 12/31/16

Expand learning beyond the printed book. Download free, complementary educational resources for this book from our website, www.lerneresource.com.

Table of Contents

St. Patrick's Day

St. Patrick's Day is a holiday.

It is March 17.

St. Patrick lived in Ireland.

He was a religious man.

People in Ireland

celebrate St. Patrick.

Other countries

celebrate too.

Everyone can enjoy

St. Patrick's Day.

This parade is in Japan.

Cities have special celebrations.

Chicago is a city in Illinois.

People there turn the Chicago

River green.

Why do you think they turn the river green on St. Patrick's Day?

11

Cities hold parades.

New York City has the

biggest one.

Dancers perform

Irish dances.

Green is a color of Ireland.

Ireland's flag has green on it.

People wear green on

St. Patrick's Day.

People also decorate with green.

Shamrocks are an Irish symbol.

Corned beef and cabbage are popular Irish foods. People like to eat them on St. Patrick's Day.

What other Irish foods might you eat on St. Patrick's Day?

St. Patrick's Day is fun.

It is about celebrating

anything Irish.

How do you celebrate St. Patrick's Day?

St. Patrick's Day Symbols

shamrock

Irish flag

pot of gold

corned beef and cabbage

green clothing

Picture Glossary

flag

a patterned cloth that stands for a country

holiday

a day to celebrate

parade

an event that happens on the streets to celebrate a special day

shamrocks

small green plants with three or four leaves

23

Index

Read More

Landau, Elaine. *What Is St. Patrick's Day?* Berkeley Heights, NJ: Enslow Publishing, 2011.

Lindeen, Mary. *St. Patrick's Day.* Chicago: Norwood House Press, 2016.

Sebra, Richard. *It's Valentine's Day!* Minneapolis: Lerner Publications, 2017.

Photo Credits